THE
EAGLE
LADY

Published by

Eagle Eye
Pictures

P. O. Box 241392 Anchorage, Alaska 99524

ISBN 978-0-97435-250-3

Printed in China

Additional copies available by contacting the publisher.

Published by
Eagle Eye Pictures
P. O. Box 241392
Anchorage, Alaska 99524
(907) 745-1950
www.caryanderson.com

T H E
E A G L E
L A D Y

Jean Keene

By Cary Anderson

A long finger of land, known as the Homer Spit, juts out into Alaska's Kachemak Bay. From here, you can marvel at a jagged horizon of snow-capped mountains, inhale a brisk ocean breeze and watch waves lapping on the beach. You may witness a passing whale or a flock of shorebirds. If you are lucky, you may glimpse "The Eagle Lady."

The Homer Spit on Alaska's Kenai Peninsula stretches 5 miles out into Kachemak Bay.

A flock of rock sandpipers flies near the beach on the Homer Spit.

Eighty-three year old Jean Keene is the Eagle Lady. Better known by her nickname than her real name, Jean has become legendary. But unlike many legends, the story of the Eagle Lady is unembellished.

Jean lives modestly in a small mobile home surrounded by a driftwood decorated fence at the Homer Spit Campground. Her yard is ornamented with fishing floats, clam shells, whale bones and snow shoes. A caribou antler, a rusty, antique saw blade and several bird houses adorn her storage shed. A broken weathervane and a tattered Alaska flag testify to the storms that can brutally lash the Spit.

◀ *Jean doles fish heads from a barrel on a cold January morning.*

▶ *Eagles that are normally unapproachable seem to know that Jean is their friend.*

▶ *Fishing floats, netting and a scallop shell decorate the fence in Jean's yard.*

The seeds of Jean's notoriety were planted on a gusty winter day more than 20 years ago, when she spotted a pair of bald eagles standing on the gravel beach near her home. Jean had always maintained a feeder stocked with sunflower seeds for wild birds. Sparrows, finches and other small migratory birds were regular visitors, but eagles coming so near was unusual.

Perhaps, Jean thought, the eagles might like something to eat. Since she worked at a nearby fish processing facility where salmon and cod scraps were plentiful, she had a steady supply of eagle food. Jean took home some leftover fish which she tossed over her short fence to the eagles. The eagles eagerly devoured them.

"It all started with just a few fish heads in a bucket and 2 eagles," recalls Jean, "and it grew from there." The following day the eagles returned and she offered them more fish.

◄ *Common redpolls congregate on an old weathervane in Jean's yard.*

▶ *Bald eagles in a snowstorm anxiously await Jean.*

Tossing fish to the pair of eagles evolved into a morning ritual during that winter in the late 1970s. By the end of the first winter, a half dozen eagles were showing up at Jean's place for breakfast.

When spring arrived and people began to fill the Homer Spit Campground, the eagles disappeared. As another winter approached, the campground was again abandoned and the eagles returned. Jean resumed feeding. In a matter of a several weeks, more than a dozen eagles were arriving each morning. Jean fed them throughout the winter. As before, the eagles departed in spring.

◄ *An eagle comes in to land at Jean's place.*

▶ *Eagles reflect in a rainwater pond near Jean's yard.*

▲ *An eagle soars among the clouds.*

▶ *A council of eagles, 21 in all, waits patiently for Jean to begin feeding.*

The pattern continued; eagles arrived in winter and departed in spring. Each year, the number of eagles increased. Within 7 years, more than a hundred eagles were homing-in on the Eagle Lady's generosity. Like squadrons of warplanes, eagles flew in from the distant shores of Kachemak Bay. They came from miles around. Other fish-eating birds, including ravens and gulls, also gathered for the feast.

After 10 years, Jean was attracting more than 200 eagles. All of them were there because of her generous handouts of fish. It was as if the birds had been spreading the news among themselves. The morning arrival of so many eagles at the Homer Spit campground became a phenomenon.

To keep pace with the rising demand for eagle food, Jean brought home more and more surplus fish from the seafood plant. Some of the fish was freezer-burned after months of cold storage, but the eagles didn't mind. "I hate to see anything go to waste," says Jean, "not when someone can use it."

Jean's morning routine slowly evolved from a minor chore into a strenuous job. By the mid 1980s, Jean was no longer doling out mere buckets of fish. She was serving up scraps of salmon, herring, cod and halibut by the barrel.

Getting fish for the eagles meant working after hours at Icicle Seafoods in preparation for the next morning. With permission, she drove the company forklift to retrieve giant containers of fish from the company's room-sized freezers. Then she transferred the fish by hand into smaller, more manageable barrels.

Jean rolls a barrel of fish into the back of her truck in preparation for a morning of eagle feeding.

A real eagle stands atop a wooden eagle sculpture on the roof of Jean's tool shed.

Jean loaded the barrels into her rusty Ford pickup and drove the short distance home. She off-loaded the plastic barrels into her yard, then brandished a butcher knife and hatchet to cut the large fish into fist-sized pieces. The small chunks, says Jean, are easier to throw. And, they are easier for the eagles to carry off. Some eagles prefer to fly away with the food rather than risk having it stolen by another eagle in the feeding area.

The amount of fish that Jean manually collects and distributes is difficult to fathom. On average, Jean distributes more than 50-thousand pounds of salmon, halibut, rockfish, cod and herring to the eagles during winter and early spring. It works out to about 500 pounds per day. Ravens, crows and gulls eat some, but most of it is eaten by the eagles.

▲ *Eagles take up every available perch.*

▶ *Eagles arrive for the morning feast even on the snowiest winter days.*

▲▶ *Visitors park their cars in the campground to watch Jean and her eagles at feeding time.*

▶▶ *Unless invited inside Jean's fenced yard, spectators are asked to stay in their cars so the birds won't be disturbed.*

Eagle attendance on the Homer Spit has fluctuated, but typically 200 to 300 eagles fly in for Jean's fish breakfast. At times the count is higher. Weather seems to affect the number of eagles; the colder the winter, the higher the eagle count.

Curious people arrive, too. They pull up in cars and vans, drive-in theater style, to watch Jean feeding the eagles. Cameras poke out of car windows to zoom in on the action. Long telephoto lenses really aren't needed here. Jean sometimes tosses fish near the parking area–when it is safe–to make sure visitors get an intimate view. Eagles often feed just a few feet away from parked vehicles.

For those planning to visit the campground in winter when eagles are present, Jean enforces a simple rule: *Stay in your car.* "The eagles are not afraid to come in close while people are sitting in their cars," says Jean. "But when people get out, it causes the eagles to get nervous. A lot of the birds will take off." Many will not return until the next day.

Professional and amateur photographers from throughout the U.S. and abroad come to the Homer Spit Campground to capture eagles on film. Some shoot from their car windows, while others contact Jean in advance for permission to work from behind the fence in her yard.

Ripley's — Believe It or Not!

"A CONGREGATION of BIRDS"
"EAGLE LADY"

JEAN KEENE HAS FED A FLOCK of OVER **300 BALD EAGLES** NEAR HER HOME in Homer Spit, Alaska, EVERY MORNING for THE LAST 20 YEARS!

▲ *Ripley's Believe It Or Not! is among many publications around the world that have covered Jean's story.*

Jean's eagle feeding activity gives photographers a chance to capture wild eagle portraits and in-flight action shots, close-up. All she asks for in return is some help with fish hauling, snow shoveling or yard clean-up.

Readers of this book probably have already seen eagle images captured at Jean's place without realizing it. Jean's eagles have been featured in books, magazines, calendars, post cards and advertisements around the country. The birds have appeared on freeway billboards and on giant banners at major sporting events. In recent years, an estimated 80% of all bald eagle images published worldwide have originated from Jean's yard or parking lot.

Occasionally, media attention has been focused on Jean as much as the eagles. Stories about the Eagle Lady have appeared in numerous newspapers and periodicals including *People Magazine*, *Life*, and *Ripley's Believe It Or Not!*

▶ *Eagles come from miles around to eat at Jean's.*

Thousands of people have traveled to the Homer Spit to photograph the eagles or merely watch in awe as the Eagle Lady caters fish to her feathered friends. Jean's avian eccentricity is well-known in Alaska and beyond, but most are unaware of her past, or even where she came from.

Born October 20, 1923, Jean grew up on a dairy farm in Aitkin, Minnesota where she tended livestock and assisted her family with various chores. She was the oldest among three sisters and a brother. By the time she was 13, Jean was herding, feeding and milking cows and was a member of the 4-H Club. She was also the proud owner of her first saddle horse.

◀ *Jean chats with photographer Gary Shultz of Alaska, while Frank Lukasseck of Germany and Hank de Boer of The Netherlands shoot pictures from within Jean's yard.*

▶ *Jean's early years were spent on a family farm where she learned to ride and train horses.*

Jean taught her horse, named "Ace," to bow on command and to play dead. She had a knack for horse breaking and training which eventually led her to train horses for others. Jean would own several horses in her life, but an Arabian gelding named Flinder helped to turn her equestrian talent into a livelihood.

In 1952, Jean and her horse were inseparable. They dashed around the rural Minnesota countryside developing agility and a mutual trust. When the Red River Rodeo announced it was searching for a trick rider, the team of Jean and Flinder were quick to apply. After some auditioning and interviewing, the two joined the traveling rodeo.

Jean acquired a western-style wardrobe, custom-tailored by a good friend, then added an extra flourish to her act. She dyed her horse's mane and tail to match her own fiery red hair. Jean's dazzling showmanship thrilled audiences as she performed acrobatics on the back of her galloping horse.

Life on the road with the traveling rodeo took Jean to several states and parts of Canada. The rodeo circuit gave her a chance to hobnob with notable celebrities including cowboy singer and actor, Gene Autry, who was once one of America's biggest stars. The daredevil Jean Keene was becoming well known, too. Her career in the saddle was about to hit the big time.

▲ *A rodeo daredevil in the making.*

▶ *Known as "The Singing Cowboy," Gene Autry was among the celebrities Jean met on the rodeo circuit.*

Upcoming performances included a major rodeo show at Madison Square Garden in New York City. Jean was really looking forward to it. "Wow," she thought, "it doesn't get any bigger than that." Her rodeo cowgirl life style was as glamorous as it was fun. At the same time, it was treacherous.

Thrills and spills are a fact of rodeo life. One afternoon during a show in Detroit, Michigan, Jean was performing one of her dangerous stunts on horseback at the Olympia Arena. In a maneuver called the "death drag," she leaned back in the saddle a fraction of an inch too far; just far enough to miss a critical hand hold. Jean tumbled backward off her horse and slammed her head against the arena wall.

Fans in the bleachers let out a gasp, but Jean couldn't hear it. She had been knocked unconscious. To make the drama worse, her right foot was caught in a stirrup as she dangled upside down behind her running horse. Jean's left leg was being battered between the horse's rear legs. A startled crowd watched as Jean's limp body was bounced and dragged around the dusty arena.

Fellow rodeo performers sprinted to Jean's rescue. They stopped the horse and freed Jean's leg from the stirrup. Jean was sprawled motionless in the dirt while her colleagues tried unsuccessfully to revive her. The ambulance, always on standby for such emergencies, zipped across the oval center field with its red lights flashing.

▲ *Jean and a friend's horse each enjoy a bottle of Coca-Cola inside the Jolly Chef Truck Stop in Minneapolis.*

Local press covered Jean's career-ending rodeo accident. (Her maiden name appears in the newspaper caption.)

Jean performing on horseback.

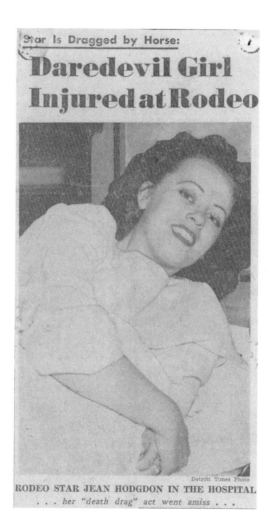

Star Is Dragged by Horse:

Daredevil Girl Injured at Rodeo

RODEO STAR JEAN HODGDON IN THE HOSPITAL
. . . her "death drag" act went amiss . . .

Paramedics strapped Jean onto a gurney and wheeled her on board. As the ambulance sped away, Jean awakened to a blaring siren. Noticing the uniformed paramedic beside her, she sensed she was in the back of an ambulance, but she wasn't sure why. Her first words after regaining consciousness were, "Hey, what happened?"

On arrival at the hospital, doctors and nurses examined Jean thoroughly and gave her some good news. Her head injuries were not serious. But there was some bad news. "Your left knee," a doctor calmly explained, "is broken in 15 places." After surgery to pin her knee back together, Jean spent months in recovery, immobilized with a plaster cast from the waist down.

The tragic accident appeared in the headlines of local newspapers while Jean rested in her hospital bed.

A split-second miscalculation in the rodeo arena had changed Jean's life. She would be lucky enough to walk again, but her mistake marked a solemn end to an exhilarating career.

Jean was forced by the injuries to find another line of work. Her scheduled performance at Madison Square Garden would never happen. She still rode horses, but not with the showy, wild abandon of her rodeo days. Jean sought employment outside the rodeo spotlight. Still a cowgirl at heart, she used her farm experience and combined it with truck driving to land a job transporting cattle.

Even though driving trucks was considered a male occupation, Jean was not deterred. At the time, she was one of only a handful of women across the country employed as a professional truck driver. Her skill with driving big trucks later led Jean to become a school bus driver.

By the early 1960s, Jean had married and divorced. As a single mom with a young child named Lonnie, she had little time to reflect on the recent past. The need to support her son, combined with her love of animals, inspired her to open a dog and cat grooming business. She also raised and bred English cocker spaniels.

"I really like animals," says Jean, "and they seem to like me." Always patient and caring toward her customer's pets—no matter how ill-mannered some of them were—Jean tried to make friends. Suffering an occasional dog or cat bite was one of the occupational hazards, says Jean. "I groomed the pets that no one else would groom."

To get by, Jean often worked long hours. This was especially true when she owned and operated a small café in Minneapolis called the Jolly Chef Truck Stop. As owner, Jean seldom took time off. Trucks continued to roll in as hungry drivers took a break from behind the wheel. Jean served them hot coffee and meals, 7 days a week.

▲ *Pouring coffee at the Jolly Chef Truck Stop in Minneapolis.*

◀ *Jean pursues a new career as a truck driver hauling cattle.*

Jean first traveled to Alaska in the early 1970s to attend the wedding of her cousin, Layne St. John. Like many who visit the state, she was awed by the breathtaking scenery. "I loved the mountains, the ocean and the wildlife," she says. It was Jean's first taste of Alaska, a land where grizzly bears roam the backcountry, moose wallow in roadside ponds and caribou migrate on the open tundra.

Few places exist in the world, says Jean, where you can stroll a beach and watch a sea otter floating on its back and eating a clam, while a bald eagle soars overhead. On summer nights, the sun stays up. On dark winter nights, the mysterious northern lights glow in hues of green and red across the sky. When Jean returned to Minnesota, she couldn't stop thinking about Alaska.

▲ *A soaring eagle.*

◀ *A sea otter floats on his back.*

▶ *The magnificent aurora borealis shines above an Alaska river.*

▲ *A moose drinks from a roadside pond.*

▶ *A bull caribou wanders the autumn tundra.*

After several trips to the state, including some with her son, Jean was hooked. She wanted to live in Alaska. Lonnie was 17, old enough to make up his own mind about moving north. He decided to stay in Minneapolis where he grew up. The decision for Jean, who has described herself as "half-Gypsy and half-Indian," was emotional, yet clear. She packed all her belongings into a secondhand motorhome and headed north toward a new life.

The road from Minnesota to Alaska is about 3,600 miles long. Jean drove for 7 days. "Most of the road in northern Canada and Alaska—about 15-hundred miles worth—was dirt. It was still unpaved," she remembers, "so it was pretty rough going." But other than bumpy terrain and a lot of nervous contemplation about her future in Alaska, the lengthy trip was uneventful.

▶ *A grizzly bear wanders across a wide-open valley.*

Jean ended up in the Kenai Peninsula town of Homer, a place well-known for its scenic grandeur and its halibut fishing. On arrival in the spring of 1977, she found a job at Icicle Seafoods, a fish processing plant on the Homer Spit. Fresh and frozen seafood is packed at the plant for shipment around the world. The job entailed long hours and required direct contact with lots of fish guts and slime, but Jean has never been afraid to get her hands dirty.

Jean parked her motorhome at the Homer Spit Campground, conveniently close to her new job. She had no idea how long she would stay. The wheels on her small home have not rolled since. This beachfront spot, with a spectacular postcard view of the mountains and sea, is where Jean has remained.

In the summer when the eagles are away, Jean's fenced yard is surrounded by Alaska tourists that fill the Homer Spit campground with travel trailers and tents.

◀ *A sign by the road into town confirms the great fishing to be found in Homer. (Sign art by Faron Steele.)*

▲ *A large stained glass window adorns the foyer at the Homer post office. (Window created by the 1987 stained glass class at Kenai Peninsula College, Kachemak Bay Branch.)*

▶ *Some local businesses display eagles on their signs, like this one designed by Guff Sherman.*

By late fall, seasonal visitors disappear and leave the campground barren. The Land's End Resort at the end of the spit remains open to a limited, mostly local clientele, but nearby souvenir shops and charter boat offices are closed for the season.

Winter is the time of year when Jean Keene gets busiest being the Eagle Lady. Throughout the summer and fall, Jean quietly collects tons of eagle food to last through the busy feeding season. She often stores the fish for months in the deep freeze facilities at Alaska Bait and Ice. As winter approaches, Jean uses her truck–which is equipped with a tow strap–to gather and arrange heavy driftwood logs for the eagles to perch on.

Land's End Resort, where Jean is a regular, is open year round. The restaurant menu there features a drink named in Jean's honor, the Cafe Keene.

Jean strolls the Homer Spit beach.

In late December, another season of eagle feeding begins without ceremony. A half-hour before the sun strains over the eastern mountain peaks, Jean sits quietly in her motorhome sipping a mug of decaf in dim lamp light. She watches her yard through small windows that are stained with dried sea spray.

Eagles arrive and land on the beach and on the driftwood just outside. Some of the birds land atop Jean's motorhome. They make a distinctive sound, like a bass drum, on her metal roof. "I can tell the difference between the eagles and other birds when they land up there," Jean says. "The eagles have a heavy thump."

▶ *Eagles gather near the surf.*

◀ *Eagles sit atop Jean's home.*

▶ *A regal eagle flies with gulls.*

Eagles perch atop the Harbor View Boardwalk sign.

An eagle sits on Jean's rusty old Ford pickup.

Many of the eagles position themselves a block or more away. They pick a vantage point that allows them to see when Jean begins feeding. Some wait on nearby rooftops. Some perch on business signs by the road. Others sit atop street lights. One eagle likes to sit on the hood of Jean's rusty old Ford pickup.

Just after sunrise, Jean pulls on her Carhartt coveralls that are stained with fish blood and speckled with silvery scales. She cracks open the door of her motorhome and steps out. Shrieks of eagles, the cries of gulls and the caws of crows punctuate the crisp morning air. Even from a distance, the birds seem to recognize the Eagle Lady. Jean recognizes a few of them, too.

▶ *An eagle stands watch from the roof of Boardwalk Fish & Chips on the Homer Spit.*

*An eagle lands atop
a street light on the
Homer Spit.*

*An eagle gazes sternly
from a stump near
Jean's yard.*

Distinguishing between one eagle and the next is difficult, but some of them are unique. "Pirate" has a crippled right foot. "Ta-wo-ha" has a deformed beak. "Betsy" is uncommonly tame and often perches on the fence a few feet from Jean. "I think Betsy spent part of her life in captivity," she speculates.

Walking slowly out into her yard, Jean pauses near her fence to lift the lid off a barrel she has readied the previous afternoon. The morning show begins. Birds start circling overhead and gathering nearby when the Eagle Lady starts to toss fish.

◀ *A handful of herring.*

◀ *Jean's favorite eagle, Betsy.*

▶ *An eagle quickly turns and swoops on a windy day at Jean's place.*

▼ *An eagle cries out to announce his presence in the feeding area.*

Dozens of eagles fill the air awaiting their turn to swoop on the fish as it hits the frozen ground.

Jean throws some fish atop her motorhome where several waiting eagles scramble to claim it. More eagles wait patiently atop a tall driftwood snag. Jean flings a herring upward and one of the birds leaps from the snag to catch it with its talons, midair. The feeding of the eagles lasts more than an hour.

After Jean is finished with hand-distributing the fish, eagles soar above and dot the landscape within a quarter mile of her beachfront home. When the eagles have had their fill, many spend the remainder of the day resting on driftwood. Some sit atop the Salty Dawg Lighthouse, a famous local landmark. Others perch atop the masts of fishing boats in the nearby harbor. Eagles are everywhere.

Cinematographer William Bacon III takes aim at two eagles from atop a refrigerator in Jean's yard. For safety reasons, Jean no longer permits climbing on objects in her yard.

A pair of eagles atop the Salty Dawg lighthouse, a famous landmark on the Homer Spit.

Eagles loiter on a semi near Jean's place.

An eagle keeps watch over the Homer Spit from high atop a crane.

The distinct plumage of an immature bald eagle is displayed in flight.

Throughout the afternoon, the eagles gradually disperse. By nightfall, all have left the Homer Spit to roost in the spruce and cottonwood trees throughout Kachemak Bay. They will return the next morning to share in the quarter ton of fish that Jean offers up each winter day.

From January through mid-April, Jean persists through wind-driven rain, snow blizzards and sub-zero weather to dutifully feed the eagles. The eagles expect her to be there and she has never disappointed them. When frostbite injured one of her toes during a severe cold snap, she carried on with little complaint. Only one occasion has caused Jean to miss a few days of eagle feeding.

In the winter of 1994, Jean was told she had breast cancer. On the advice of Dr. Paul Sayer of Homer, surgeons performed a mastectomy. But not before Jean made prior arrangements for the eagles. A friend was hired to feed them during her brief absence. After just 3 days, she was feeding the eagles again with some help.

◀ *A tall mast makes a good vantage point for an eagle in Homer's boat harbor.*

▶ *An eagle rests on rocks on the Homer Spit.*

◀ *An eagle perches on a caribou antler attached to Jean's tool shed.*

▼ *An eagle prepares to swallow a herring, whole.*

Within a week, Jean was back to her solo eagle feeding routine. "I'm a tough old bird," she once told TV newsman Jerry Bowen. In his coverage of the Eagle Lady for the CBS Evening News, Bowen concluded that Jean was "perhaps, the toughest bird of them all."

Jean's devotion to the eagles has sometimes extended to injured or sick birds. On rare occasions, she captures an eagle that has been wounded by an animal trap or other mishap. Such birds are usually delivered to Dr. James Scott, an Alaska veterinarian and eagle specialist. He cares for them at the Bird Treatment and Learning Center in Anchorage until they are well enough to be returned to their natural habitat.

One year, Jean spotted and captured an eagle that had accidently flown face-first into a cable. The collision peeled back the white feathers on the left side of the bird's head. So ghastly was the bird's left profile with festering, swelling and bleeding that the caretakers at the treatment center dubbed him "Frankenstein."

▲ *With assistance from her nephew, Scott Kempf, Jean rescues an injured eagle.*

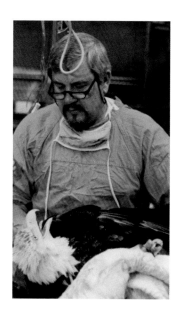

▲ *Dr. James Scott tends to an injured eagle in his operating room.*

53

The name, Frankenstein, wasn't befitting an eagle, so Jean secretly changed it. "That was a horrible name," she thought. The last word came when Jean was honored to release the rehabilitated bird back to the wild. With its head healed and its white feathers beginning to fill back in, Jean set the eagle free with its new name, "Spirit Dancer."

Jean cares passionately about the eagles that greet her each winter morning. But every spring the birds go their separate way. They return to catching prey.

Bald eagles in Alaska, like eagles elsewhere in the United States, eat all types of fish and a variety of small mammals, including rabbits, mice and squirrels. They also eat ducks and other birds.

◀ *An eagle with ruffled feathers.*

▶ *Eagles gather at the end of the spit on the beach near Jean's place.*

Eagles prey on almost anything they are agile enough to catch. They also scavenge on the carcasses of moose, deer, seals and beached whales—whatever they find that has died. Scavenging is a beneficial trait that helps to rid the environment of rotting flesh, which could cause disease if allowed to sit indefinitely.

The eagle's superior eyesight is its greatest asset when searching for food. Its high-powered eyes are among the best in the animal world. An eagle's eyesight is several times sharper than a human's. It has been said that an eagle can spot a fish up to 3 miles away. One study suggests that an eagle can identify another airborne eagle at an incredible distance of 40 miles.

◀ *An eagle's piercing eyes.*

▶ *Relaxing on a branch.*

The primary tools used by an eagle to catch its prey are its feet, which are equipped with needle sharp claws or "talons." The rough bottoms of its feet and its strong grip are well-suited for struggling prey. Even slippery fish find it difficult to escape.

An eagle must be quick and clever to survive, but to insure the survival of its species, it must find a mate and reproduce. Spring and summer are the seasons for the eagles to build nests and raise young.

An eagle snatches a fish from the water.

An eagle feeds a trio of nestlings.

▲ *Eagles in the treeless Aleutian Islands of Alaska must nest on grassy ridges or on rocky cliffs, as shown on the facing page.* ▶

Most eagles gather sticks and twigs to build their nests in trees, but some prefer the face of a rocky cliff. In Alaska's Aleutian Islands where there are no trees, eagles often nest on the ground surrounded by tall grass.

Eagles usually lay 1 to 3 eggs. Baby eagles, called "eaglets," emerge from their shell in about 5 weeks. After hatching, the fuzzy young birds are constantly tended by one of the parents while the other searches for food. The male and female adults take turns feeding the chicks and guarding the nest. Within only 8 weeks, the fast growing eaglets develop feathers and change in color from light gray to dark brown.

After the eaglets are feathered, they begin to exercise their wing muscles. They hop up and down flapping their wings until they are eventually ready to fly away from the nest. Their first attempts at flight often end with clumsy, crash landings, but the young birds quickly become skilled flyers.

▲ *The bald eagle is common in Native American culture as in this wood carving in Ketchikan by Nathan Jackson.*

◄ *The eagle has made numerous appearances on U.S. postage stamps.*

By the summer's end, the fledgling eagles have learned to hunt and scavenge for themselves. They are still brown colored, but will soon develop some white markings. They won't acquire a fully white head and tail until they reach adulthood at about 5 years old.

The adult bald eagle, known for its striking good looks, has long been symbolized by Native American culture in a variety of art forms including masks and totem poles. The bird was chosen as the national symbol of the United States in 1782 and its image can be found on numerous postage stamps, coins and currency. Eagles are also featured in advertisements for a wide variety of American products.

Throughout our nation's history, an assortment of coins and bills have featured an eagle on the reverse side.

Bald eagles can be found patrolling the skies throughout North America, but Alaska has more of the majestic birds than any other state. In fact, Alaska has more bald eagles than all other states combined. Alaska is the only state where the bird has never been listed as threatened or endangered.

While the Alaska eagles that visit Jean are still away for the summer, the Eagle Lady stays busy on the Homer Spit. Although Jean has retired from her job at the seafood plant, she stays in touch with plant managers and local commercial fishermen. They know she gathers and stores tons of fish to feed the birds in winter, so they keep her and the eagles in mind when surplus fish becomes available.

Sometimes, Jean goes fishing for salmon and halibut in Kachemak Bay to satisfy her own taste for seafood. Most days, she stays at home and tends her colorful garden. She is passionate about flowers and fills her entire yard with them.

◀ *A pair of eagles is silhouetted as a fishing boat passes by the Homer Spit.*

▶ *An avid gardener, Jean tends to a yard full of flowers in summer when the eagles are away.*

◀ *An eagle sits atop a pile of logs on the Homer Spit.*

▲ *Eagles joust for a favorite perch in Jean's back yard.*

▶ *A pair of eagles rests on a pair of pilings on the beach at Homer.*

As cool autumn breezes arrive and Jean's flower garden begins to wither away, she starts thinking of the eagles that will faithfully return for her morning banquet.

When winter settles in, Jean ventures out at sunrise to hand out barrels of fish and her eagle feeding season begins anew. Hundreds of eagles gather near her home in a fascinating, annual spectacle on the Homer Spit.

It's a sure sign of winter in Alaska, when the eagles return once again to meet their long time friend,

THE EAGLE LADY

◀ *An eagle sits atop a salmon-shaped sign at sunrise and waits for Jean to serve breakfast.*

▲ *An eagle sits on a storage trailer next to a weathervane in Jean's yard.*

▶ *A portrait of Jean's hands and her silver eagle ring.*

Acknowledgments

Special appreciation is due the following people for supplying fish, encouragement or a friendly hand over the years: Icicle Seafoods, Don Giles, Rob Rogers, Ralph Carstens, Charlie Roberts, Jon Faulkner, Peggy & John Chapple III, Kenny Quinn, Al & Jan Waddell, Jeff Wraley, Steve Tarola, Robin Brandt, Scott & Jane Kempf, Alan Schulz, Tom Mangelsen, Howard Buffett, Tom Walker, Steven Kazlowski, Preston Cook and Mike Wallace. Thanks to members of the U.S. Fish & Wildlife Service for assistance in capturing injured birds.

Thank you also to Connie Taylor of Fathom Graphics for her layout expertise, office equipment and crucial advice; Ralph Talmont of Barkfire Press for his assistance with the cover; Erling and Eileen Johansen for proof-reading; Joe Nedland of Nedland Design & Illustration for the book's finishing touches; Dennis Douglas of Anchor Point for his generous accommodations; fellow photographer Dave Parkhurst of Alaska Naturally for his helpfulness in discussing the project —sometimes at 3 in the morning; and Ellen Anderson for her faith, love and support.

This book is dedicated to
Jean's son, Lonnie, and granddaughter, Chelsea.

About the Author

A writer, photographer and broadcaster, Cary Anderson has covered news and features for some of the world's leading media organizations. His photo credits include *National Geographic*, *Newsweek*, *Outdoor Photographer*, *The New York Times*, *Popular Photography*, *Astronomy* and many other publications. He has written and narrated well over a thousand reports for the *CBS Radio Network*.

Anderson's other books include *Valley of the Eagles*, *Alaska's Magnificent Eagles* and *Aurora, A Celebration of the Northern Lights*.

▲ *Author Cary Anderson watches for wildlife at Tern Lake on the Kenai Peninsula*

▶ *An eagle rests on a driftwood stump near Jean's place.*

Contributors

Additional images and copyright permissions generously provided by the following photographers: Photo on page 15 by Ellen Anderson. Photo (left) on page 53 by Jasper James. Photo of author by David V. Allen.

Archival photos and clippings courtesy of Jean Keene. *Ripley's Believe It Or Not!* cartoon used with permission of Ripley Entertainment, Inc.